Sonja & Maria Kofelenz
with
Patrick O'Hara

The Two of Us on the West Highland Way

Our hiking experiences in Scotland

Reutte, August 2019

*Bibliografische Information der Deutschen Nationalbibliothek:
Die Deutsche Nationalbibliothek verzeichnet diese Publikation in der Deutschen Nationalbibliografie; detaillierte bibliografische Daten sind im Internet über http://dnb.dnb.de abrufbar.*

© 2019 Sonja & Maria Kofelenz

*Text: Sonja Kofelenz
Translation: Patrick O'Hara
Satz: Sonja Kofelenz
Fotos: Sonja & Maria Kofelenz
Maps: Patrick O'Hara*

Production and Publisher: BoD-Books on Demand, Norderstedt - Printed in Germany

ISBN: 9783743166318

The book is also available as e-book.

For

Patrick O'Hara

and our friends
Nicole, John, Sean, Blanaid and Emer

Preface

Sonja: I walked the West Highland Way with my daughter Maria. It led us along small country roads, wide forest roads and old military roads, along small streams, along paths through heather and pastures to our destination at Fort William.

The course required a certain endurance and fitness, but always rewarded us with a breath-taking landscape.

Maria: I walked the West Highland Way with my mother. While we enjoyed some hours of sunshine, we often had to walk in drizzle or heavy rain, over hill and dale, through mist and, at times, in very humid air. After 10 days we arrived, satisfied and happy, in sunshine in Fort William.

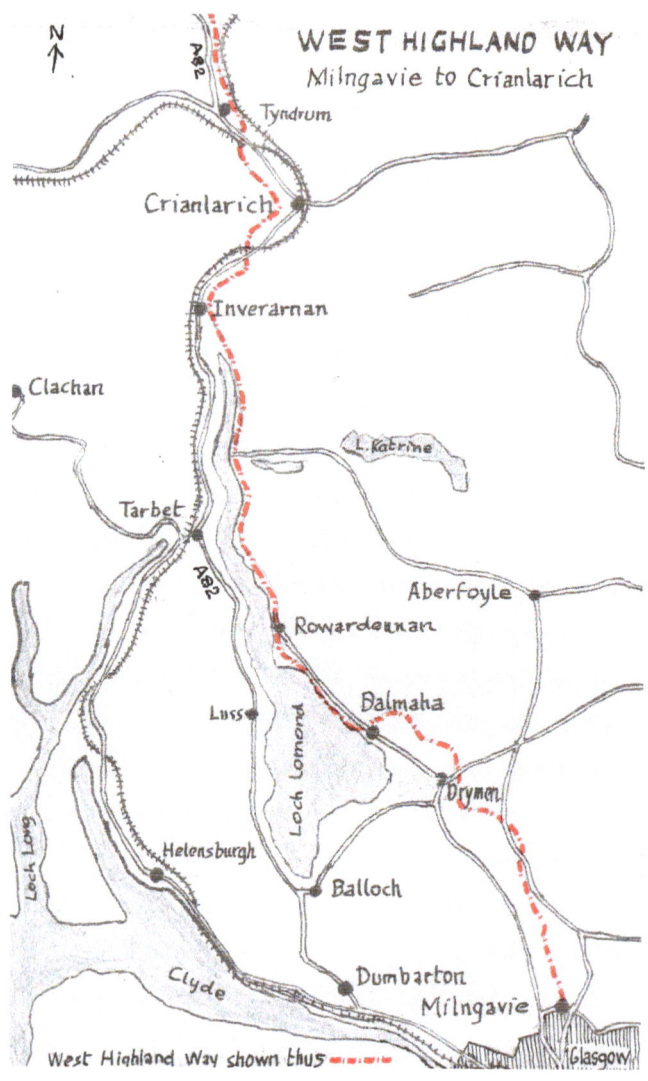

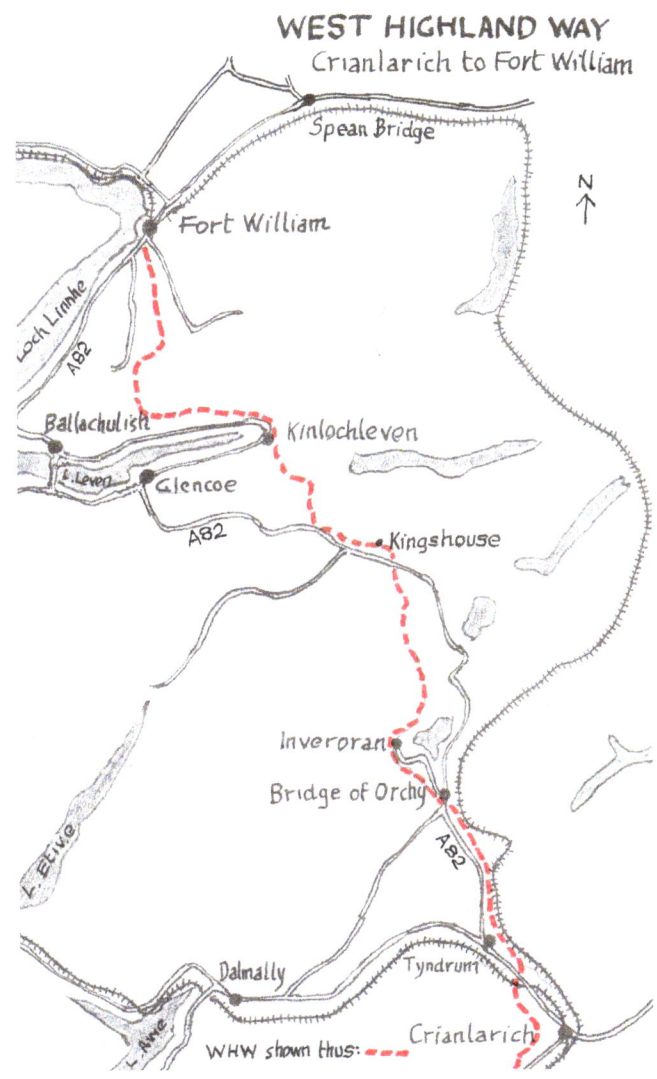

The West Highland Way

The West Highland Way is Scotland's first official long-distance hiking trail, opened in 1980. It stretches from Milngavie, a suburb of Glasgow, to Fort William, a distance of 154 km.

The starting point is in the Lowlands and the route goes northwards through a constantly-changing landscape. The highest elevation is at the Devil´s Staircase (584 m).

The trail can be followed all year round. Every year about 50,000 hikers come to take on and enjoy the challenge. Most of the West Highland Way runs along many old roads, mostly livestock routes, military roads and old makeshift roads. The symbol of a stylized white thistle in a white hexagon serves as a landmark and can be easily recognized everywhere.

Most hikers take the route from south to north so that they will have the sun (when it shines) behind them and will not be blinded by it.

The two of us - on the West Highland Way

Why should a mother and daughter want to do such a long hike together? I can think of several reasons. One was my ulterior motive of helping my daughter to improve her English. I also saw it as an opportunity for the two of us to holiday together; such an opportunity might not arise again as Maria grew older.

The dream of the long-distance hiking trail had been haunting my mind for some time and so I thought this was the chance. One needs sufficient free time to undertake such a route. While this would not be a problem for me I could not leave my seventeen-year-old daughter at home alone while I was absent. So I decided that Maria had to come with me. I planned the individual stages of the walk to suit us both.

Maria would have preferred to go to Australia, but unfortunately our travel budget was not big enough. Although we had been to Scotland four times already, Maria was happy to go there again. We both like hiking and there would be plenty of interesting things to see and a lot of nice things to eat. Backpacking seemed like adventure. So we decided to take it on.

Here, dear readers, you will find a short description of both of us:

At the time of the trip, Maria was seventeen years old and still attending high school in Reutte. In her free time she surfed the internet, painted her fingernails three times a week and now and then accompanied me on excursions or walks.

We both have a passion for books but we did not expect to find many bookstores in which to browse on this particular trip. My love of books is probably due to my job: I am a librarian and therefore extremely precise and conscientious. I have many hobbies: Gardening, hiking, running, knitting, cooking, reading.... I rarely get bored.

Before Christmas there was a guide to the Highland Way on our living room table and it was studied in detail. A distance of 154 km had to be covered. I made myself a list of questions viz.:

- **How do we get there?**

- **What´s it going to cost?**

- **What distance can I expect my daughter to travel each day?**

- **Where do we sleep?**

First we had to decide which travel time was best and then make the necessary arrangements for travel and accommodation. The studied guide recommended spring or autumn. These times did not suit us, because Maria was attending school. So we only had the summer months.

In order to avoid the notorious Scottish midges as far as possible, I decided to do our hike in late August and early September. To Maria's delight the dates I chose meant that Maria got two extra days of holidays from school.

The next question to be decided was: how long would it take us to complete this walk?

The guide indicated that, at a fast pace, the route could be completed in 5 days but that seven days would enable it to be done in a more relaxed way.

It was, however, clear to me that even seven days would be too fast for Maria and me. We would not be able to do the daily distances required. So we decided to plan for two weeks and got the OK from my husband to leave him, my son Marcus and our two cats for this period.

Harry Potter included

Sometimes Maria sits giggling on the sofa in the living room. During a car journey she constantly bursts out laughing. At home, she leans on the kitchen table and eagerly types on her tablet PC. When you ask her what she is doing, she gives a growl or an angry look. One - especially Mom - disturbs. And this has been going on for more than a year. When I ask her what she is doing that is so important, she says she is reading something or writing a story.

Do you know what this means? It's the Harry Potter fever. She and her girlfriend in Munich, with whom she is always in contact via Internet, are totally addicted to the stories of the magic student. However, the books and films are no longer enough for the two of them; they attack every Internet blog and read every further story written by others. No, still not enough! They invent new events around Hogwarts, rewrite the stories and turn them upside down.

If Maria is in a good mood, then I get one or the other story read out to me, whether I like it or not. One night, she told me that parts of the Harry Potter movies were shot in Scotland. Well, that was not news to me, as I had been dealing with the Harry Potter books and films for a few years before she became aware of them.

Leafing through my newly acquired hiking guide, I proudly presented Maria with information about the Jacobite Train. This old steam locomotive which travels between Fort William and Mallaig, became "The Hogwarts Express" in the Harry Potter movies. It passes features known from the films such as the

Glenfinnan Monument and the long viaduct with 21 arches.

„Mom, do you think we can go on the train?" Maria asked immediately. „No, Maria, we will probably only have time to look at it. But if we walk well and have a day to spare, then we'll travel on it!" And so it happened that we were able to add another highlight to the crowning finale of our tour.

Route planning with small hurdles

The first thing I did was to divide the route into manageable stages. That was not so easy, because at the end of each stage we would need a place to stay. With the help of our guide book, a map and the internet I set to work. Soon I had finished the division, ensuring that a longer day's walk would be followed by a shorter one. I even managed to plan a "rest day" and the promised extra day for "train travel". The next major decision we had to make was the choice of accommodation. Should we make our way puristically with a tent? That would certainly be the cheaper option. Or would we prefer a room with washing facilities and above all a room in which to dry off and warm up after a rainy day?

Having already been in Scotland three times and distrusting the weather conditions there, we decided on the more expensive option. This, of course, required us to have a precise timetable. When the endpoints were determined, I went looking for affordable accommodation, sending off emails in my rather simple English.

Soon the answers arrived - and to my great joy I received no refusals. The variety of our accommodation was quite colourful - from the simple youth hostel, to a so-called Home of Hobbits, to guesthouses for Bed & Breakfast and up to the luxury of a hotel. Prices ranged from £ 40 a night to £ 100 in a hotel-room for two. Unfortunately, in some places there was no alternative to booking a hotel room. Booking, in some cases, required a little effort as I had to make telephone calls to provide my credit card details. I proudly told Maria afterwards that I had made telephone calls to Scotland and, despite my difficulty in speaking English, had succeeded in arranging all our accommodation.

Yes, the fitness... and then came Pokemon to Go

A distance of 154 km should not be underestimated. In the Spring I told Maria that we should train a little bit for it. I had already thought up a training plan. At first, a walk only once a week, towards summer twice a week and in August I wanted to drag Maria along the Lechweg, our local long-distance hiking trail. But it wasn't that easy to motivate her.

I did, however, manage to persuade her to come on a little mountain tour or hike almost every weekend. So we worked our way up to various alpine huts and also completed a section of the Lechweg. At the very top of the Lech Valley, in Vorarlberg, we explored the Lech springs and the Steinerne Meer. I succeeded in luring her there with a new piece of sports equipment; got us both a pair of 5-Finger-Shoes. With these we climbed through the Steinerne Meer. As its name suggests, it is a seabed raised by tectonics, a wild landscape.

Unfortunately, my ambitious fitness plans did not fully work and I slowly got a bit worried about our ability to complete the Highland Way.

To add to the uncertainty, in mid-July my son Marcus brought home for Maria and myself a new mobile phone app, a game called Pokemon to Go. It hit like a bomb. Following its arrival, my daughter´s attitude to physical activity changed abruptly. Now she preferred to "run" kilometre after kilometre through our village in any weather, in order to catch "beasts".

What do we put in the backpack?

As the departure date slowly approached, I began to write a list of what we should take with us. How much could we carry? Last year I bought a large backpack, intended to be used on my first long-distance hiking trail, which I did not start. In the meantime, the backpack has served as a transport container for various local festivals.

My husband Werner now provided Maria with a large touring backpack (for ski tours). As my backpack was quite capacious, I realised that it could easily become too heavy to carry over long distances. So I set the limit at 10 kg and packed only what was absolutely necessary.

The following is a list of what we decided to bring for each:

Sleeping bag of small packing size
Rain cover for the backpack
Flip-flops for indoor use
5-Finger-Shoes
Plastic bag with clothing
(3 underpants, 2 T-shirts, a spare pair of trousers, 3 pairs of socks, 1 fleece jacket, 1 rain jacket)

1 small towel
Hat, headband, scarf
Hiking sticks
Toiletries (in miniature form)
First aid kit, sewing kit and tape
Knife, plastic bags, some string
Some cereal bars
1 thermos flask
Mobile phone + charger
Notepad, ballpoint pen

Avoiding any unnecessary duplication, we divided our belongings between the two backpacks. In Maria´s came her toiletries, her clothes, her flip-flops, rain protection for the backpack, on top, her sleeping bag and her rain jacket. The rest was stored in my backpack, which had a final weight of 10 kg. Maria, whose backpack weighted only 5 kg, promised to take a turn from time to time in carrying my heavier one.

The time had finally come! We looked forward to spending the next 14 days in Scotland.

Saturday, 27.8.2016

Arrival day!

At 4:00 in the morning the alarm clock rings, our adventure begins. Papa Werner takes us to the airport in Munich, where we arrive at 6:30 am. Our luggage - our two backpacks with all the straps sticking out - was packed in two large black garbage bags.

These were not strong enough and the bags already had holes when they were loaded into the car. On Werner's advice, we put both packs into a large ice hockey bag for check-in. After checking in our luggage, we say goodbye to Werner and go through security and customs. In the departure area we have a small breakfast and then go to the departure gate.

Our plane leaves at 8:30 am and we arrive in Glasgow at 9:45 am local time (10.45 am in Austria). During the flight we meet several people who have the same destination. Most of them are already in hiking clothes and studying guide books for the Highland Way. At the baggage carousel at Glasgow Airport we pick up our large ice hockey bag. But what should we do with this huge bag?

First we look for the right bus to take us to the Central Station in the city centre and have our first experience of the Scottish locals and their strong Glasgow accents. When we are safely on the right bus, it takes about 20 minutes to reach the station. There we look for the luggage storage to park our ice-hockey bag for the next two weeks. A policeman directs us to it but we find that storage is out of the question for cost reasons. The baggage handler tells us that we would have to pay about 70 pounds for the two weeks. That is definitely too much for our budget.

Before making a decision, we buy our tickets to Milngavie (pronounced "Mallgay"), a suburb of Glasgow and the starting point of the West Highland Way, at an online terminal. Standing around this counter, a beggar asks us for money. So it occurs to us that, to help this man, we should offer him our bag which we would otherwise have disposed of in a garbage bin. After praising the bag, he gladly accepts it.

Now it's getting exciting! Which train do we have to take to Milngavie? The station is quite big and there are many tracks. Our destination does not appear on the departure displays, so we have to ask at the service counter. There we learn when and where the next train leaves and we look for our platform. We don´t have to wait long and after 25 minutes we arrive in Milngavie. From the train station it takes only 5 minutes to get to the centre of Milngavie. First we look for a supermarket and stock up with a snack for tomorrow and a lunch for now. On the shelf I discover a wonderful beer that I recognise from past holidays in Scotland and take a bottle with me. While we eat our sandwiches on a bench in a nearby park, familiar faces from the airplane pass us, carrying their backpacks. Maria is very tired; she did not sleep the night before and takes a nap on the park bench. But at two we set off to look for our first guest-house.

We arrive at the B&B Best Foot Forward in a side street and are received there by the very nice host. After welcoming us, he informs us about the breakfast that awaits us tomorrow, about the sights along the hiking trail and the eating possibilities in Milngavie in the evening. He takes our order for breakfast and then shows us our room. We have a four-bed room with private bathroom. Quite tired after our journey we sleep until the evening and then set out for one of the recommended restaurants. We end up in a typical Scottish pub, where we celebrate our first evening with a burger for Maria and an ale pie for me.

On this occasion Maria receives a premature birthday present from me, which she is very happy about. I present her with her ticket for the Hogwarts Express, the Jacobite Train in Fort William, wrapped in a gift roll. But that, of course, will have to wait until we finish our long walk.

After a good dinner we go back to our guest-house and retire to bed early.

Milngavie

Milngavie is a suburb of Glasgow, 13 km from its centre. But you won´t find any urban flair here. Milngavie seemed to be a little sleepy place.

In the centre, which is the pedestrian zone on Douglas Street, you will find several shops, cafés and restaurants. There are rows of single-storey houses which create the impression of a village. The pedestrian zone decorated with flower pots, lanterns and benches, invites you to have a stroll around, but once you leave this area, the rest of the place looks quite modest. Low blocks of flats without green areas, a lot of concrete buildings in front of the station and, in between them, some single-family houses with beautifully laid out gardens.

There are few locals about, but many hikers who have chosen Milngavie as a starting point for the West Highland Way or other walks in the surrounding area.

Sunday: 28. 8. 2016
Milngavie - Drymen (19.2 km)

At 8:00 o'clock we arrive in the breakfast room of the B&B and are pleased to find a well-decorated table. There is even a miniature Austrian flag to show that the table is ours. We help ourselves to fruit juice and cornflakes. Each of us receives, as ordered the evening before, a plate of fresh, scrambled egg and several slices of finely smoked Scottish salmon. A good start to the holiday. Now we also get to see our landlady who warns us to watch out for modern highwaymen during our walk. But I´ll come back to that later.

At 9:30 am we make our way to the official starting point, which is located in the pedestrian zone in Milngavie directly next to the stone bridge over the Allander Water River. At the stone column with the West Highland Way logo we meet a man from Baden-Württemberg, who is so nice and takes a photo of to two of us.

From the starting point we descend a staircase down the side of the bridge, cross a car park and continue along the Allander Water River through light deciduous forests. Many old oak trees can be found here. The path takes us upwards into Allander Park, and then leads us into Mugdock Wood, a large recreational area with beautiful hiking trails and rare plants, such as sundew. We cross a road at the end of the forest and reach a wetland with small, shallow lakes, the Craigallian Loch and the Carbeth Loch. Like jewels, both are covered in swamp vegetation, grasses and perennials with colourful berries. The path is lined with blackberries and raspberries, which I can´t resist nibbling.

Shortly after Carbeth, just as our landlady had warned, we met a number of unkempt people loitering around an old shepherd's cottage. They seemed quite drunk and were approaching passing hikers to tell them sad stories and say that they are collecting donations for a charitable organization. It is quite obvious that any donations given will be used for their beverage supply. One of their stories concerns the dog they have with them. According to them, it´s half a wolf. But we heeded the warning and walked past them, saying that we must hurry on.

Our path leads over hilly grassland. Now and then we see sheep. According to our guidebook the Gumgoyach Standing Stones should now be on the right side of a hill. Despite an exhaustive search, we discover only one rock that protrudes diagonally from the fern. At Dumgoyach Farm we cross the river Blane Water, turn left and follow a railway line for a long time.

A highlight on this route is certainly the Glengoyne Distillery, which we reach at noon. In front of the building we have a picnic, aerate our boots and enjoy a dram (a little sip) of whisky in the shop. We put a very small bottle in my backpack.

We spot a Bavarian hiker, whom we had met on the plane, as he arrives in a taxi. We are very surprised as he had told us that he intended to walk the whole route to Fort William in a very short time and later do another long-distance hiking trail.

At Glengoyne we changed into our 5-Finger-Shoes. Our hiking boots had become too hot. The track is smooth enough to allow us walk in our light footwear.

The day is warm, but the air is humid. It rains for a while, but we continue to walk in T-shirts.

There are many cows and sheep to be seen in this area. We also see a great variety of birds, including pheasants and jays. The hedges have plenty of berries, many having the most beautiful shades of red. They provide us with a snack.

For a while we have the man from Baden-Württemberg as a companion. Maria and I refer to him as "Würti" as we still do not know his name. He leaves us shortly before Drymen, because he wants to set up camp on a camping site there.

On this first stage there are also quite a few bikers whom we have to be careful to avoid as they pass. At Gartness we pass the Wishingwell Farmhouse. This is a large farm with coffee shop, souvenir shop, beer garden and a camping site. Not surpisingly, many hikers take a break here. But we move on.

Shortly after the farm we cross a salmon river on a large old stone bridge. Near the bridge the river flows over the typical steps which enable the salmon to leap up to their spawning area. No fish to be seen today.

Maria has no problems with this first distance of 19.2 km, as I feared that she might. However, we are both very happy when we find our accommodation in Drymen after a long search. Our hostess assigns us a tiny room and explains the lay-out of the kitchen two floors below. She suggests that we might prefer to have breakfast at the inn across the road from her house if we wish; however, we can make breakfast for ourselves in the kitchen where coffee, tea and different kinds of cereals are available.

After showering and rubbing with various toiletries, such as marmot oil cream and stone oil lotion, we rest awhile. We have to share a bathroom with an Asian couple. You have to get used to the fact that strangers use the same bathroom.

As the oldest pub in Scotland is claimed to be in Drymen, we naturally want to honour it with a visit. With fresh ale, a hellishly spicy lamb dish for me and a tasty burger for Maria, we end a pleasant evening. On the way home to our little room we pay a visit to the local shop and buy sandwiches for the next day. By 8 o'clock we are in bed.

Breakfast at B&B Best Foot Forward

River Allander Water

Bridge over the River Blane Water

Glengoyne Distillery

The Glengoyne Distillery

At the foot of a small hilltop, Dumgoyne Hill, stand the white buildings of the whisky distillery, which was founded by George Connell in 1833.

Ian Macleod Distillers Ltd. has been the owner since 2003, making it one of the few Scottish family-owned distilleries. In earlier times this area was in the hands of bandits who operated numerous illegal distilleries.

This distillery, with three stills, produces 1.2 million litres of whisky annually. The 10- and 17-year-old Glengoyne whiskies tested by us have a sweet, floral taste and are not peaty. The whisky is aged exclusively in American and Spanish oak barrels in which sherry was previously matured. These barrels colour the whisky which would otherwise look like water.

Monday: 29. 8. 2016
Drymen - Balmaha (11.3 km)

After our self-prepared breakfast, consisting of a bowl of cornflakes, a large cup of instant coffee for me and thin cocoa for Maria, we wait in our room to use the shared bathroom. When we finally arrive packed and backpacked down in the kitchen, we pay cash for our room and march off. At 9:30 am we are at the point where we left the West Highland Way yesterday.

The weather is fine as we start the second stage of our route. We found out that it made good sense to tape our feet at the problem areas before the start. This helps to avoid blisters. Maria is more at risk of blisters than I am. She drinks a lot of water on the way from the bottles which we filled before leaving our room. The water tastes of chlorine.

The route leads along a path beside the main road through beautiful farmland; we see again today a pheasant on a pasture. Shortly after a B&B, the path turns off towards Garadhban Forest and after a short ascent, lined by countless broom bushes, we reach the forest. We follow the forest road for several kilometres. Often, looking back, we have a wonderful view of the wide valley through which we passed yesterday. The path leads us slightly uphill after a crossroads and the forest ends after 1 km. This is where the heathland begins.

We see sheep, some standing beside each other behind isolated bushes, others resting in grass hollows. We cross several small streams rushing with marshy water. From here we can already see Conic Hill, which we will cross today. The path leading up the flank of the mountain is easily visible from a distance. Several hikers with their colourful jackets and backpacks are on the way up.

We rest at the foot of a beautiful waterfall below a bridge. Removing our footwear we enjoy cooling our feet in the water. We decide to have lunch here before we climb Conic Hill (358 feet) and unpack our sandwiches. A short time later Würti appears and joins us while we eat.

A long ridge leads us upwards on the hill, through flowering heather and broom. For the first and only time we meet some Highland cattle with their shaggy fur and long horns. They stand in the middle of the track and refuse to move aside. Carefully we sneak past. The well-trodden path leads us higher and higher and offers again and again fantastic views into gentle side valleys. Just below the summit we take a sip of "summit whisky" as a reward. Maria doesn't want to go all the way to the summit, so I have to climb the last 20 metres on my own. From the top I have wonderful views over the whole area, Loch Lomond stretching away to the north and, to the south, the route we have followed from Drymen. That's remarkable!

After a short rest, we start the steep descent to Balmaha, which turns out to be quite difficult because of the many steps, boulders and rocks. Shortly before the village we pass through a beautiful high forest. The sun is shining and it is very hot.

At 14:30 we are on the bank of Loch Lomond in Balmaha and move into our room in a bunkhouse near Balmaha House.

The bunkhouse is a developed barn, and the overnight stay is cheap. The house is divided into several small rooms with simple single beds or bunk beds in 4-bed rooms. There is a shared bathroom and a lounge with kitchen. The room is much bigger than our room in Drymen and the people are also very nice. We can make breakfast ourselves again: the necessary food is all there, even toast, butter and jam.

After the usual showering, rubbing and relaxing we go to the nearby Oak Tree Inn for dinner. I have a pint of ale on the terrace first. I then have haddock in beer batter with chips while Maria has another burger. After this filling (and, to my mind, very fattening) dinner we walk back to our quarters, call home and go to bed.

The route to Garadhban Forest

Great view on a hilltop

The way up to Conic Hill

A backward glance - how far we have come!

From the top of Conic Hill

The best Fish & Chips we ever had

Tuesday, 30.8.2016

Balmaha - Rowardennan (12.5 km)

At 7:30 a.m. we make our breakfast in the kitchen. We boil water for tea or coffee and find bowls for muesli. Plates, cutlery and cornflakes are on the table. In the fridge we find fresh milk, butter, jam and bread for toasting. Shortly afterwards, people come into the kitchen from the other rooms. It is a group of young people from London with whom we have a good chat.
On their recommendation we try Cereal-Bars. They dissolve in milk and form a pulp. It's really not my thing - it tastes like softened cardboard that I have to choke down. Maria has the same experience with her cornflakes. I prefer a slice of toast, but I have problems with the toaster and end up with some charred slices with jam on them.

Like yesterday, we are ready to leave at 9.30 a.m. and collect the deposit for the room key from the landlord.

Today's route is quite simple. We go northwards along the eastern side of Loch Lomond. Shortly after the small pier of Balmaha we climb a hill called Craigie Fort. From above we have a fine view over the Loch. The path now passes close to it and we pass beautiful pebble beaches. Dense oak forests board the shore, which is strewn with boulders between gravel and sand strips. On this part of the trail there are also several camping sites with shopping facilities for hikers and, thankfully, a toilet.

Shortly after the entrance to Cashel Farm we reach a road, which we follow for about 2 km. At Sallochy Cottage a path leads us back to the shore and takes us to Ross Wood, which lies on a peninsula jutting out into the Loch. We have to climb three small hills and, at the highest point, we reward ourselves with a sip of whisky. This usually inspires Maria and so she is the first to arrive at the top.

On one of the hilltops we make friends with a robin we call Cheddar. The little guy jumps up close to our backpacks and watches us eat our lunch. Of course he gets some - he likes cheddar cheese.

As we continue, we notice quite a few of these pretty birds.

From Ross Wood we reach a lower area with larch, bushes and many mushrooms.

At 2:30 pm we hit the road just before the hotel at Rowardennan, walk past it and find the youth hostel 500 m further on. It is an old castle, surrounded by a wonderful garden. We get a nice, large room; adjacent to it are the sanitary facilities and the dining room.

After registering, we order dinner for the evening meal and lunch packages for tomorrow. Then follow our usual routine of showering and rubbing. As we have a lot of time until dinner, we go to the lounge with its open fireplace, internet, comfortable leather sofas and large windows overlooking Loch Lomond.

It is like a salon in a castle. We make ourselves comfortable there, reading our books and enjoying some ale.

At dinner we discuss our route for tomorrow - it will be one of the longest and most strenuous days of our walk and will finish far beyond the northern end of Loch Lomond.

We had hoped that there might have been a ferry to shorten our journey up the Loch but found that there wasn´t any suitable one. To make tomorrow's route a little easier for us, we organize transport for the larger rucksack. This facility is offered cheaply at each of our overnight stops. It´s quite simple; I fill out a form, indicate when and where the backpack should be delivered and pay £ 7. It´s worth it to us, so all we have to do is wear the raincoats and bring a snack in the smaller rucksack.

A stone bench near Blair Burn

At the crossing at Cashel Farm

Our robin „Cheddar"

The Rowardennan Lodge Youth Hostel

Wednesday, 31.8.2016

Rowardennan - Inverarnan (22 km)

As discussed the day before, we get up early to be on the track in time. Today we have 22 km ahead of us. After a substantial breakfast, we clean our room, put the bed linen into the container and pack our backpacks, this time a little differently. Everything we don't need on the way goes in the big backpack. We take only the most important things with us: snacks, drinks, rain jackets, bandages, money and documents. We attach the luggage tag to the large rucksack with the address where it should land and deposit it in the hut where it will be collected for transporting. With a faint worry that we might not ever see our beloved rucksack again, we go on our way.

At the reception we receive the packed lunch - sufficient for two days.

At 8:30 am we start in light rain, which lasts the whole day. We decide to follow the alternative route indicated in the guide. The official route along the banks of Loch Lomond is not recommended, especially in the rain. On a wide forest road, which provides us with fine views of the Loch, we make good progress. After approx. 7 km the alternative route meets ours again. The forest road ends at a turning point, from where a beautiful path continues along the shore and we walk through colourful oak forests. By noon, we cross a bridge to reach

Inversnaid. The bridge spans a raging torrent of water falling down, over several cascades, from Loch Arklet to Loch Lomond. There is a lovely hotel at Inversnaid, where we delay only long enough to enjoy a hot chocolate.

Small groups of hikers arrive at the bar while we are there. Some of them take off their shoes to relieve sore feet. Food is available but we will wait to have our wonderful packed lunch later.

As Wi-Fi is available here (we have not had it for two days) we send photos home and to our friends. Among the incoming emails I find one from the Drovers Inn in Inverarnan enquiring whether we still want to have the room we booked for to-night (if not, they would give it to others). I guess I´ll have to call so we can get a roof over our heads for the night.

We leave at 1 pm. On the way I call the Inn (which is a little difficult with my rudimentary English) and confirm that we expect to arrive around 5 pm. We now have one less thing to worry about.

From the Inversnaid Hotel the West Highland Way is very challenging. For about 6 km we follow the shore but have to climb over hills, some quite steep and sometimes over large rocks. It takes its toll in time and energy.

The smell of goats is very strong in this area due to the wild goats who live here. We hear them, but we don´t see them.

Maria has great fun poking her walking stick again and again into many of the delicate plant cushions which we find along our way, with almost diabolical giggling as she does so.

We cross rivers and rivulets coming down the slope to our right. Only a few hikers are on the way. Usually we stomp along without talking to each other, the only noise being the sound of the wind and of the water lapping on the shore of the lake. It´s very meditative to march like that. Occasionally the sun breaks through briefly, but is quickly followed by dullness and drizzle. It is warm in the humid air and we each wear only a T-shirt and a light rain jacket. In the backpack we have our snack, that´s all we need.

After crossing the Allt Rostan, the path becomes easier. We reach a bay with a beautiful gravel beach lined with willows. We are now at the northern end of Loch Lomond and entering agricultural land. Crossings and gates demarcate pastures and soon we see the remains of the old Doune Farm. One of the buildings is now used as a bothy, which provides basic accommodation free of charge. Inside the bothy is a large room with an open fireplace, platforms on the left and right for sleeping and, in the middle, a table with material for making a fire. We imagine what it would be like to spend the night here. With a flickering, warming fire and in the company of other hikers it should be very comfortable.

At 4 pm we go through a small pass and reach a plateau with swampy vegetation and a small lake, Loch Geal. All we hear here is the wind. We drop down into a valley, where we reach Beinglas Farm and a large camping site. We cross a bridge over the River Falloch which flows southwards into Loch Lomond and a short road-walk takes us to our hotel at Inverarnan, the "Drovers Inn".

It is an ancient building, in a lovely location. The interior is decorated with old hunting trophies, rusty swords and stuffed animals. The portraits on the walls are of an indifferent quality. Our room is a spacious one on the top floor with comfortable beds; the rest of the furniture is very shabby. There is only one bathroom with toilet on this floor, which we share with the occupants of four other rooms. This bathroom probably dates from the 1920's and is in moss green with no shower only a bath.

After we have taken a bath, we sit down in the bar. It has an old, dusty ambience with dark tables and chairs and a tired, tartan carpet. The waitresses are friendly and there is a warm jovial atmosphere with many hikers and other visitors at the bar. We enjoy a great dinner with Guinness Steak Pie and Prawns & Chips. Maria gets her beloved Chocolate Fudge Cake with cream. Hm... Then a short call home and off to bed.

Some good things on the way

Bridge over Snaid Burn

The way to Doune Bothy

Maria climbs some rocks

The lobby of Inverarnan Drovers Inn

Our bathroom - to share with other rooms

Thursday, 1.9.2016
Inverarnan - Crianlarich (10.6 km)

Since we have a shorter distance ahead of us today, we get up later. In our ancient bath we freshen up and go down to the bar for breakfast. It is already very full but we squeeze into a small table. After we identify ourselves as residents, we are handed the cooked breakfast menu and choose fried eggs with bacon and fried egg with ham. They put a toast holder filled with white and brown toast on the table and we help ourselves at the buffet with juice and cornflakes. In the dining area we find the usual mixture of tourists and hikers. They are clearly recognizable by the footwear; most of them are sitting in hiking socks at the table. After this ample breakfast we pack our backpacks. From here to Kinlochleven we must carry our entire luggage ourselves.

After taking a few photos of this worthseeing hotel, we start the 5th stage. We hike back on the A82 to Beinglas Farm, there we get sandwiches in the camping shop and off we go.

The path leads us through Glen Falloch, close to the rushing river of the same name and the beautiful Falls of Falloch.

Rivers in Scotland, and also the lakes, should not be imagined as having the pure clarity of the mountain streams where their water originates. As the streams flow downwards through boggy areas, the water takes on a brownish hue like diluted Coke and has a peaty taste.

Again and again we meet hikers who were sitting near to us at breakfast in the "Drovers Inn". We recognise a father and a son who follows him with obvious reluctance. The son walks with a water bottle in one hand and a mobile phone in the other. There is no conversation between them. Later, after they have passed us, we see the son resting on a rock, red-faced from the effort of keeping up with his father. How different to Maria and myself. Even if our feet are burning, the straps on our shoulders are hurting and we are perspiring in our jackets, we always have fun and find amusing things on the way. We laugh as we have to crawl under the railway line through a shaft tunnel. Most other hikers are quite silent.

After this underpass we find a sheltered spot for lunch, out of the wind which is strong today. We spread out our garbage bags on damp moss and sit on them while we eat our sandwiches and drink tea. Soon afterwards we are joined by a young girl with a huge camera and a big backpack. We have difficulty conversing in English but when I ask Maria "How do you translate Hochspannungsmast?" we are delighted to discover that the young lady actually speaks German. Her name is Aischa and she accompanies us the rest of our journey to the youth hostel in Crianlarich.

The path now leads steadily upwards on an old 18th century military road. Below us a wide valley spreads out and behind the wall, which borders the path on the valley side, we can see many sheep. Shortly before we come to Crianlarich we reach a pasture fence where the path forks. On the right it leads into the village and on the left the West Highland Way continues uphill. We go to the right and walk downhill through spruce forest towards the youth hostel. In the forest we take photographs of red mushrooms which are growing here in masses.

We arrive at the youth hostel quite early. To future hikers on the West Highland Way we can definitely recommend this hostel; clean, modern, good sanitary facilities and large rooms. In the evening we sit in the lounge to read and meet a London group we previously met in Balmaha. We tell each other how things have gone so far.

The only drawback at the youth hostel was the food on offer. The frozen ready meals are not recommended and we decide to go to a pub tomorrow. Alternatively, you can use the well-equipped kitchen and cook something for yourself. We also make extensive use of the opportunity to wash our clothes. Everything we are not wearing, we put into the washing machine. That was urgently needed. Because of all the sweating and the high humidity our things are very smelly. Our washed clothes dried very well overnight in the drying room.

WHW through Glen Falloch

The tunnel under the railway

Sonja on the West Highland Way

Crianlarich Youth Hostel

The trails along the West Highland Way:

For half of the way we walked on beautiful forest roads and old military roads. These former military roads date from the time when Scotland was occupied by the English. In order to be able to intervene quickly when problems arose, the English built roads across the country so that troops and carriages could be moved rapidly. Today, these wide paths, similar to our forest roads, often with rough stones but firm underground, are used as hiking trails and are pleasant to walk along.

There were also mountain tracks and trails, which usually led us through heath and moorland. Most of the trails which led us over passes and hilltops were in good condition. When it was raining, we found that small shallow streams had formed, even on high ground. Even though we had a period of bad weather, we were not disappointed. As we had noticed during previous stays in Scotland, it can sometimes be very warm and summery there. But as the Scots themselves say, that´s Scottish weather for you! Unpredictable!

Every now and then the paths were muddy but we usually managed to avoid getting our boots too dirty by stepping carefully on stones or wooden planks. Occasionally we had to use a tarmac road (e.g. when crossing the A82 or for a short distance near a village) sharing the road with traffic, always keeping in mind that the British drive on the left.

As described in our hiking guide, 4500 vertical metres had to be climbed over a distance of 154 km. The ascents were all moderate and the total climb is spread over the whole length of the journey. However, one should not venture completely unprepared on a long-distance hiking trail but should plan the individual stages well. Our longest stage (the last one) was 24 km long and called for endurance. On average we walked for 4 hours a day. The longest stretch took 8 hours without breaks. For long stages one should start early to avoid finishing too late in the evening, especially when the days are short.

Friday, 2.9.2016

Crianlarich - Tyndrum (10.7 km)

Before breakfast, I write my diary entries for the day before. Then we go to the breakfast buffet and select toast, jam and yoghurt. After breakfast, we pick up the laundry from the drying room. It is lovely to put on fresh clothes again.

We are ready to leave at 9.30 am. In the shop around the corner we buy only two sandwiches, having still some other supplies. I had already filled our flask with tea and the bottles with water in the hostel kitchen.

First we go uphill to the turnoff for the WHW. There we meet a German couple who had camped on the hilltop. They´re spreading their belongings out on the wall to dry. It rained heavily during the night and everything got wet.

Now the path, covered with many red mushrooms, runs slightly upwards through a beautiful coniferous forest. Most of the trees are spruce or larch. Open ground is covered with heather, interspersed with many berry perennials. During a short breather, some midges attack us, so that we do not delay, despite the beauty of the place. We spray ourselves thoroughly with insect repellent and then have some relief from the pests.

The path goes up and down through dense forest and has small bridges where it crosses over streams. Passing under an imposing railway viaduct we reach the valley of the River Fillan and drop down to the A82 which we cross a few hundred metres later. A wide road over farmland brings us to Kirkton Farm. There we find, as described in the guidebook, a small old cemetery and the ruins of the chapel of Saint Fillan. To our great surprise, we find that our friend from Baden-Württemberg (whom we thought we had left behind us) has got here before us. After a short exchange, we sit down at the side of the road on two concrete pipes and have a snack.

On the wide path we make good progress and pass the Auchtertyre Farm with its restaurant, pets corner and shop. Many other hikers stop here, but we continue along the small river Fillan until shortly before Tyndrum. We leave the river and forest road and, following the West Highland Way symbol, are led over a hilltop, in the middle of a wonderfully blooming heath landscape. From the top we can see a small lake, a feast for the eyes. A stone bench has a commemorative plaque of a sunken sword.

Back down from the hilltop we come to a wide footpath, interrupted by a high cattle gate, which leads into a forest with old trees. A notice tells us that there used to be lead mining in this area. The few remains of the mine can still be seen as well as a large bare area devoid of vegetation.

A few hundred metres further on, we arrive at the Tyndrum camping site, where one of the Hobbit houses is waiting for us. These small, barrel-shaped wooden houses are quite spacious inside. Ours has one large bed and two smaller ones, refrigerator, microwave, heating and TV. In the facilities block right next door to our house, are the showers and toilets as well as a kitchen. Soon we make our way to the pub with Aischa, whom we meet again at the reception. We each have a burger and ale. Maria and Aischa share a Chocolate Fudge Cake. We then take a tour through the adjacent tourist shop to stock up on snacks.

Tyndrum is very touristy with houses offering B&B, and some hotels and campsites. Its souvenir shops are kept busy with visitors from the many coaches which make a stop here.

Our sleeping bags are used for the first time in the Hobbit house. Maria is delighted with her new one. I borrowed a similar one, but the term "sandbag" would have been more appropriate. Before use, I have to shake out the heaps of sand inside.

Some news from home: the rest of the family is busy mowing the lawn and one of our cats is missing. That´s what the chick usually does when her mother isn´t at home.

In the forest near River Fillan

Some flowers on the way

A spectacular stone bridge

Maria is looking for the right way

A small lake on Dail Righ

Our Hobbit House at Tyndrum

Saturday, 3.9.2016

Tyndrum - Inveroran Hotel (14.3 km)

In the morning it is quite cool in our Hobbit house, so we switch on the heating. Breakfast is very modest, a bottle of orange juice, tea from the day before and shortbread.

Then we collect our things again, fetch fresh water bottles in the reception and are already on the way at 9:45 am.

On the subject of packing: we have to do this every day anew. Our ritual starts at night, before we got to bed, by unpacking, covering all the storage areas of the room and hanging our jackets and hats on hooks. Maria always spreads her stuff on the floor. So the room looks pretty chaotic. In the morning, order is restored as everything goes back into the backpack in a certain order. Medication and bandages at the bottom, then the plastic bag with the clothing, the washing kit and, depending on the weather, a fleece jacket or rain jacket near the top. Topmost, of course, the most important thing: the lunch snack. Drinks and large rubbish bags for sitting on, go in the side compartments. In the pouch at the top we keep cards, money, passport, notebook and pens.

If the weather is bad we put the backpacks inside rain covers to keep the contents dry. If you are wondering where our flip-flops and sleeping bags are: they are stored in the bottom compartment. Sometimes Maria overlooks her flip-flops and has to jam them into the top pouch of her backpack. Before we finally start, we tape our feet to avoid blisters. The rest of the tape goes in my jacket pocket, in case the need arises while we are en route.

We wear the same hiking trousers every day, only changing T-shirts, socks, underwear and jacket, depending on the weather. Maria ties her hair together and fixes everything with a headscarf. I wear my hat. In the evening we treat ourselves to fresh clothes and comfortable footwear - i.e. flip-flops.

Leaving Tyndrum, we walk through the village and then turn northwards into a valley between high mountains, narrow at first but widening as we proceed. The railway line from Glasgow is close to us for most of the way to Bridge of Orchy except at one section where it curves away in a long arc to our right into Gleann Auch. There it crosses a spectacular viaduct, set against steep mountain flanks, before returning to be with us for the rest of the way to Bridge of Orchy. As the valley widens, we see sheep, cows, farmland, areas covered with heather and many waterstreams. Bridge of Orchy is a typical Highland village with few houses and a large hotel. Here we cross the A82 and the river draining southwards from Loch Tulla. Our path leads upwards, away from the road, through a beautiful young forest. At the highest point we have a wonderful view north-eastwards over Loch Tulla to

Rannoch Moor, the largest continuous moor landscape in Scotland. Except for the purring of the wind, there is a great silence now, with not a sound from the A82 as we look over this great expanse. We look forward to reaching it tomorrow.

We celebrate our arrival at this point with another "wee dram" of whisky and then drop down steeply into a wide valley and can see the Inveroran Hotel in the distance, our destination for tonight. The hotel stands alone on a small river, the Abhainn Shira, which flows eastwards into Loch Tulla, not far from the hotel. In earlier times the hotel served as a shelter for the cattle drovers.

We are warmly welcomed at the Inveroran Hotel and book a table for dinner. Our room is very large and we have our own bathroom. After refreshing, we visit the Walkers Bar to have a pint of ale before dinner. When it´s time for dinner, we go to the dining room and take a seat at our well-laid table. We can highly recommend the food here: Maria opted for a salmon steak with risotto and I for a venison pie (venison ragout) and a glass of fine red wine. Real luxury - but only what we expected at the room price. After dinner we sit in the salon and enjoy the rest of the evening.

View over Rannoch Moor

Again passing the railroad

On the top of Mam Carraigh

Inveroran Hotel

We had a fine dinner

and a relaxed evening

Holiday fund - how much our holiday cost

Prices in England and Scotland are slightly higher than in Austria or Germany. The exchange rate at the time of our trip was 1 pound sterling for 1.10 Euro. The British vote to withdraw from the EU (Brexit) had weakened sterling, giving us a better rate than we would otherwise have received. Some examples of prices:

1 pint of beer (0.6 l) in the pub cost £ 3 on average (the equivalent of 3.30 Euros.)
A ready-made sandwich, packed, in the supermarket the same amount.
1 pack of salami sliced £ 1.99

The prices of food in the supermarket were almost the same as at home. It was different with accommodation: a room in a Bed & Breakfast cost us an average of £ 60 for two people. Hotels were more expensive.

As already described at the beginning about the reasons for my choice of accommodation, we wanted to travel as comfortably as possible and have a room with shower every evening. We did not wish to stay in tents. Due to our stage destinations, however, the choice was often limited to only one type of accommodation and that was sometimes expensive. Nevertheless, in some places it was possible to stay overnight cheaply. We stayed in B&BS, inns, hotels, youth hostels and once on a camping site.

A private room (for 2 people only) in a youth hostel costs about £ 20 per person. The price includes the use of communal showers and a common room with a large kitchen for cooking.

Bed & Breakfast rooms were available from 40 pounds per room for two people up to 60 pounds. Hotels were more expensive - our most expensive was £ 100 for two for the night (a very substantial breakfast usually included). Room prices are seasonal and are higher in the high season.

The standard of the rooms we occupied in Scottish hotels and guest houses was much lower than that of similar accommodation in Austria.

Dining out in pubs or restaurants weighed heavily on my wallet. For example, we paid an average of £ 10 for a burger with fries (not these measly rolls with meat from a fast food chain, but a more than satisfying meal), a little more for a steak & ale pie (read the chapter on the wonderful food in Scotland here). Add drinks and we had dinner for an average of £ 30 for the two of us. Desserts in a restaurant cost about £ 5.

What else you do you need? Of course, a snack for hiking! Sometimes we found a supermarket or a small shop, and supplied ourselves. If neither was available, we ordered a packed lunch (£ 4 to £ 6) with mostly identical contents which was enough for 2 days. In the evening we had a beer in the pub. And to make our journey more comfortable, we twice organised transport to take the heavy luggage to our next destination; this cost £ 7 each time.

Many hikers had tents with them and camped in the wilderness, which seemed to be allowed everywhere in Scotland. One exception was on the shore of Loch Lomond - there you have to camp on designated camping grounds. We met hikers with tents who used campsites and occasionally stayed at youth hostels in order to shower and wash and dry their clothes. In this way they keep the cost of their overnight stays to a minimum. They also keep their food costs low, having camping stoves to cook their own meals. While this way of hiking has financial advantages it has the great disadvantage of increasing the weight of the loads to be carried (tent, dishes, stove, food, sleeping bag etc.).

Sunday: 4. 9. 2016
Inveroran Hotel - Kingshouse Hotel (15.7 km)

There's a luxurious meal waiting for us in the breakfast room: freshly cooked porridge, scrambled eggs with smoked salmon and fresh fruit. This would certainly be a good place for stressed managers. Besides wonderful cuisine, the hotel has well-furnished rooms but, because of its remote location, it has no reception for mobile phones and no internet. We pay for our room and receive the pre-ordered lunch package.

The composition of a packed lunch:

2 sandwiches with the filling ordered beforehand (ham/cheese, tuna salad, salami usually available)
1 bottle of water (0.5 l)
1 apple or other fruit
1 bag of potato chips (known as crisps in Scotland)
1 chocolate bar
Raisins in a small box

This is more than enough for a hungry hiker.

Shortly after leaving the hotel, we cross the Abhainn Shira by Victoria Bridge, an old stone bridge at the foot of which some hikers have pitched their tents and are about to gather up their belongings. Our path now heads northwards and steadily upwards east of the high mountains of the Black Mount area, passing along the edges of some young forests. Eventually it leads us to the western end of Rannoch Moor.

Unfortunately, the blister on one of my feet is very sore today. So I walk for a while in my 5-Finger-Shoes. When I change, I notice that the blisters have burst. I stick plasters on them which make me more comfortable. As I change footwear I notice that I have lost my woolly hat. I put it in the belt on the side of the backpack and it must have fallen off. That was my favourite hat - a great loss.

On this section we experience the full viciosness fo the Scottish midges. As soon as we stop, they attack us mercilessly. Our drinking breaks have to be short or we will be eaten alive.

When it gets a little steeper, I change back to my hiking boots and, just as I do, it starts to rain heavily. It continues until we reach the highest point of the route when the sun emerges and we have a magnificent view over Rannoch Moor. I always imagined it as a flat plain, but it is full of little hills covered in heather and, in between, small lakes glistening in sunlight and streams running and gurgling everywhere. The whole area must be of great interest to botanists, having so many species of plants including some rare orchids.

The path now leads steadily downhill across the lower slopes of Meall a´Bhuiridh and we can already see the white building of the Kingshouse Hotel in the distance. To our left now is the chairlift serving the "White Corries" ski Slope. For us Tyroleans this seems quite miserable and neglected. Nevertheless, there is a lot of traffic on the access road to the lift from the nearby main road (the A82 again). At the bottom station of the lift there is a new car park. We cross the road and head for our hotel. As we approach, we pass a large construction site and as described in the travel guide, we meet tame deer in front of the hotel. We get within two metres of them before they move away.

The hotel is by far the most expensive accommodation we have booked. So let's hope for some comfort. We get a large room with bathroom. The furnishing is antique, but all right. The bathroom has a bathtub with shower curtain; there is no mixer tap for the water. The high room price is probably due to the fact that there is no other accommodation available for some miles and the convenience of the location for walkers on the WHW, skiers using the White Corries ski slope, and mountaineers wishing to tackle the high mountains flanking nearby Glencoe.

Since we arrived very early, we make ourselves comfortable in the bar and sit for a while in the beautiful lounge, where we watch the deer from the window. We like the bar so much that we stay there for dinner and don't go into the adjoining dining room. As the evening draws in, the bar becomes crowded with hikers and the noise level rises.

Through Rannoch Moor

Soft hills and high mountains

Other hikers on the WHW

Through Rannoch Moor

It has been a long way …

Kingshouse Hotel

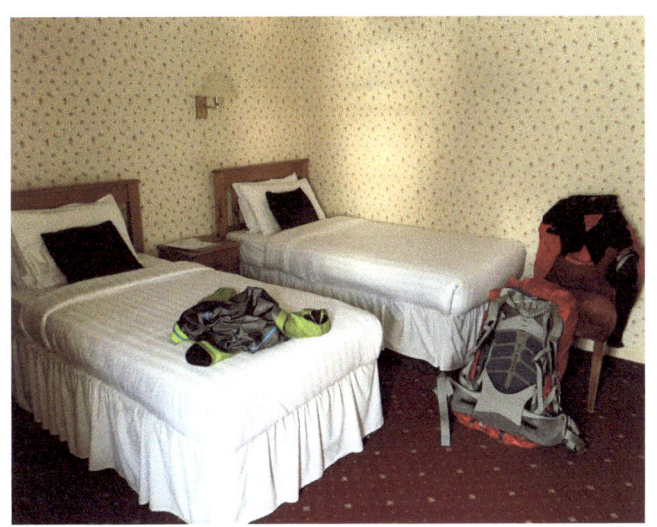

Our luxury bedroom

In the bar ... with Internet connection

Monday: 5. 9. 2016

Kingshouse Hotel - Kinlochleven (13.8 km)

We get up early because breakfast is served only until 9:30 a.m. The meal includes some delicious freshly baked croissants and marmalade. How time flies: today we will walk the penultimate stretch of our journey, which means, that we have already walked more than 100 km. As we set out, the sky is overcast as it has been almost every day. We must wear rain jackets to avoid getting wet in the damp conditions (drizzle or heavier rain). At first we follow an old military road along the lower flank of Beinn a´ Chrulaiste. We are quite close to the A82 at this stage. After a couple of kilometres we reach Altnafeadh where we leave the A82 behind us. Turning right, we head northwestwards following the old military road as it climbs steeply up through heath and moorland. There are few trees, mostly quite modest little birches. At the steepest part of the route the road forms a series of zig-zags known as the "Devil´s Staircase". We follow its many turns to reach a saddle from which it will lead us into another valley. One advantage of the bad weather is the absence of the hated midges. They don't like it and leave us largely alone. Despite the cool temperature we are sweating freely inside our jackets from the effort of carrying ourselves and our heavy backpacks up to a height of about 550 metres at the saddle. We celebrate reaching the top with a welcome whisky. Maria and I try to yodel to announce our summit victory.

We have arrived on a high plateau and enjoy a wonderful view down into the next valley. Looking back we can see the path we have taken so far today. At the top it is very quiet, only the wind purrs and the streams splash quietly.

We stomp over the plateau. We can´t take a break, because it´s not very comfortable in the rain. According to our guidebook, we are facing a steep descent, from our highest point (550 m) down to sea level at Kinlochleven (0 m). However the gradient proves to be quite moderate. Again and again we overtake the same hikers, who in turn overtake us as soon as we stop for a photo or a sip of water. At the foot of a small rock face we discover a pheasant hen with three chicks. When they see us approaching, they quickly find refuge somewhere on the rock face - too fast for us to take pictures.

Further down we reach a mixed forest, where we come along the thick pipes supplying water to Kinlochleven from the Blackwater reservoir which is on higher ground east of our path. Some of these pipes are not completely tight at the joints and a strong, spraying jet of water emerges. At the edge of the village, we pass buildings of the aluminium works, which have not been in operation for several years. Right on the roadside we arrive at our hostel, where we move into a tiny 3-bed room (a single bed and two bunk beds) for the next two days. Bathroom and toilet are off the room. We have the use of a large lounge and kitchen. After this rather wet day, we enjoy a hot shower and then finish our sandwiches.

Shortly afterwards, we visit the supermarket in the village to get provisions for today and tomorrow, including noodles and tomato sauce for this evening and milk and cornflakes for breakfast. When planning the trip, we allowed for a rest day at Kinlochleven before tackling the long, final stage.

The rest of the afternoon we spend comfortably in the lounge, reading and playing billiards. We also try a game of Scrabble, but it is quite difficult, the English version having many letters which are rather rare in the German one.

Devil´s staircase

A hard way up the Devils Staircase

Heather along the way

Near Blackwater Reservoir

Blackwater Hostel and Campsite

Tuesday: 6. 9. 2016

Rest day in Kinlochleven

Each of our beds has a sleeping bag and a quilt but the bags are not very comfortable as they have been sewn up at their ends and our feet keep pressing against their bottoms. This causes us to toss and turn quite a bit and makes it hard to sleep. We wonder how anyone taller than us can manage to get any sleep at all in such bags. In the hostel it is quite loud at night, the walls are thin and every time someone uses the toilet on the upper floor, we hear the flushing water rushing down like a torrent.

After the self-prepared breakfast I collect the laundry (which I washed quickly the day before in the sink) from the drying room. We briefly tidy up the room and then we do an inspection of the small village of Kinlochleven. It has little of interest, with almost identical houses and unkempt gardens. Our inspection doesn´t last long. After a short visit to the supermarket we sit behind the hostel in the sun and enjoy a relaxed day, recharging our batteries for the long march to come.

At noon we eat pasta with sauce and a slice of fried salmon. We spend the afternoon reading and in the evening, when it gets busy in the kitchen and all the hostellers start cooking, we make our way to the pub. We go to bed early, because we want to leave early tomorrow.

A sunny day in Kinlochleven

View over Kinlochleven

Wednesday, 7. 9. 2016

Kinlochleven - Fort William - the last stage (24.5 km)

After a modest breakfast we pack our backpacks. We ordered transport to take the heavier one to Fort William, so that we can walk faster. Filled only with the rain jackets and our snack, the small rucksack is easy to carry. Just to be on the safe side, we take the first aid kit too. Starting from sea level at Loch Leven, we have a steep ascent up to a height of 250 m. Then the terrain flattens a bit and rises gently to the highest point at 350 metres. We continue at this altitude for the next 10 km. The path takes us westwards and then turns to the north through a wide high valley covered with heather. We pass two former farmhouses, now only ruins. A break would be welcome now, but it is not possible to sit down because of the rain which brings our old friends, the midges. Only by continuing to walk can we escape them. So our sandwiches are eaten while we walk.

From Lochan Lunn da Bhra, a small lake on our left, the path goes upwards. We reach beautiful pastures with a few sheep, grazing between the heather bushes. We pass through small areas of forest and new plantations and then very large areas recently cleared of trees. In the forest it is mystical; many trees covered with moss line the pathway and mist rises.

For a short moment, a sunbeam reaches us. We pass many streams and waterfalls and reach our last high point of the West Highland Way.

Here we come to the turnoff to an Ice Age fort, Dun Deardail, and enjoy a magnificent view of Scotland's highest mountain - Ben Nevis (1344 m). The rest of the route is quite unspectacular. A wide forest path leads down to the Glen Nevis valley.

There our way meets a country road, on which we march the few remaining kilometres to Fort William. At the entrance to the town, a board proclaims: "End of the West Highland Way". This was the endpoint of the WHW until 2009, when it was decided to move the terminal point to the town centre. Tired but happy, we stroll through the pedestrian zone to the centre. We can´t really believe we´re already here. As we sit on a bench in the middle of Fort William, surrounded by other hikers who have arrived at the same time as us, my mobile phone suddenly rings. A Scottish phone number! It is our landlady of the B&B here in Fort William, who tells us that she has a water problem in the house and we can't stay overnight at her place. She offers us accommodation in another house and we accept the offer. A taxi takes ourselves and our backpacks (the large one having meanwhile arrived safely) to the Ben View Guesthouse. There we are received by two older ladies - very British. We get a beautiful room with floral motifs.

A private bathroom, also with floral decor, is included. Even the trash can is flowered.

After a lengthy shower and the pleasure of not having to put on the sweaty, strong smelling clothes any more, we went out to celebrate our successful completion of the walk. In a small restaurant Maria had her usual burger and I chose Spareribs, both enjoyed. Finally we had sumptuous desserts: Sticky Toffee Pudding and Chocolate Fudge Cake. With well-filled stomachs we tramp back on heavy feet and go to bed. When we are both lying down, we hear a train whistle from the nearby station and shortly afterwards a steam blast and the typical sound of a steam locomotive moving. I´ve never seen Maria jump out of bed so fast. She hangs half out of the window and wriggles with excitement: she has just seen the Hogwarts Express!

Tomorrow we will visit the old steam engine and travel on the train.

Mystic Forest

Farm Lairigmor - just a ruin

At the crossing to Dun Deardail

Ben Nevis

At the finish of the West Highland Way

Thursday, 8. 9. 2016
Rest day in Fort William

Our day begins with a well-prepared breakfast. We set off early for the station so as not to be late for our train. Maria is almost beside herself: she is really excited at the prospect of travelling on the "Jacobite Train", as it´s called. Proudly it stands in front of us on the rails, an old steam locomotive, painted black, with many shiny brass parts. Behind the locomotive is the tender, in which the coal is bunkered and then several carriages. We will travel in it to its terminus at the village of Mallaig. We photograph it from all sides and are allowed into the driver´s cab. There the brass levers and wheels shine and the fire is already burning in the boiler.

We take a look at the Harry Potter souvenir shop and then take our seats in the second carriage behind the locomotive. This train was used as the "Hogwarts Express" in the film version of the Harry Potter stories. Harry, the sorcerer´s apprentice, travelled on it to get to the magic school of Hogwarts.

The Jacobite Express leaves on time at 10:15. The route leads out of Fort William, over a canal with a series of locks known as Neptune´s Staircase, past harbour facilities, through an industrial area with large paper mills along the northern shore of Loch Eil. Sheep were grazing on the shore of the Loch.

Half an hour later an announcement tells us that the Glenfinnan Viaduct is now in sight. All passengers gather at the small window openings to photograph the famous structure. I succeed in taking a good photo. In Glenfinnan, a very small village with a station, the train stops for half an hour to allow passengers to visit the museum and the souvenir shop. The museum is all about the history of the construction of the Glenfinnan Viaduct. However, the museum and its shop are full of tourists, so we only stroll around the area. Since it is windy and raining quite heavily, we withdraw back into the train.

The journey continues through hilly, lushly overgrown land. From time to time a lake or stream appears. The area seems uninhabited, although we see numerous sheep and cows, especially as we get closer to the coast. The train runs without stopping through a number of small villages. At the level crossings there are always people taking pictures of the steam locomotive and waving. Punctually at 12:30 pm. we arrive at the station of Mallaig where we have a stay of one and a half hours.

First we look for a toilet and then we explore the ferry port of Mallaig which has ships serving a number of offshore islands. There are several souvenir shops, a supermarket, two fish & chip stalls and several restaurants. The restaurants are immediately invaded by passengers from our train. We discover a second hand bookstore. It magically attracts us, and how could it be otherwise for two librarians? We find many interesting books.

I buy a plush edition of "Harry Potter Snowy Owl" for Maria for her birthday. In the supermarket we get bread, ham, cheese and smoked salmon and enjoy an al fresco lunch on a bench at the harbour, watched by the greedy eyes of a seagull.

The return journey is the same as the outward journey, but without any stopover.

The train travels relatively fast, except on uphill stretches of the line when we are aware of it slowing down. In the short tunnels, the smoke from the engine envelops the carriages and the windows steam up on the outside.

Back in Fort William we get the tickets to Glasgow for tomorrow. Leaving the backpack in our room, we go shopping in the town centre. Maria wants a kilt and we find one to buy, as well as two "West Highland-Way"-T-Shirts.

The old Steamtrain „The Jacobite"

Maria in heaven!

The Glenfinnan Viaduct

The port of Mallaig

Friday, 9. 9. 2016

Fort William - Glasgow

We get up at 8 am and have a good breakfast. Afterwards we pack everything up and pay for our room in cash. We still have enough time to visit the supermarket. We spend about an hour in the nearby library, where there is free internet. Of course, the book inventory is analysed in detail. Maybe the Scots are doing a little better than we are in regard to libraries.

On the way to the station I realise that I left my hat in the room, and that despite Maria's warning: "Don´t forget your hat in the cupboard" - Unfortunately there is not enough time to go back. With a heavy heart I have to do without my second hat.

Our train leaves for Glasgow on time. The journey takes almost four hours. As the train follows the West Highland Way in places, we get glimpses of the route we walked. That´s how far we've walked!

We arrive at Glasgow Queens Street Station at 3:30 pm and have to change to another station. There are two stations in Glasgow. In the Central Station we buy the ticket to Paisley, a suburb of Glasgow near the airport. It has poured rain all day, an experience we haven´t had in the last two weeks. Arriving at Paisley station, we have to walk two kilometres through torrential rain to our accommodation. The strong gusts of wind are not very pleasant.

Dripping from head to toe, we step into the bar and are warmly welcomed by all present who tell us that to-day´s weather is typical Scottish weather. The waitress at the bar turns out to be German and hands us the room key for our amazingly inexpensive room. After we have dried ourselves and hung up our laundry in the room to dry, we return to the bar. Maria orders her last wonderful burger and I order something Mexican. The nice waitress persuades us to have a dessert we won´t regret - one delicious Chocolate Fudge Cake (what else?) for Maria and an Apple Toffee Crumble for me. We order a taxi to take us to the airport next morning and then retire to bed.

Saturday, 10. 9. 2016

The Journey Home

We have to skip breakfast in order to get to the airport in time. There are long queues at the baggage check-in and afterwards at security. In the duty free shop we get a bottle of special Scotch whisky for my husband Werner, then have a small breakfast and finally take our seats in the aircraft bound for Munich.

There we can expect the best of weather with very warm temperatures and my son who will drive us home.